GRAPHIC NOVELS

Essential Literary Genres

BY ANDREW DALE

Essential Library

An Imprint of Abdo Publishing | abdopublishing.com

ABDOPUBLISHING.COM

Published by Abdo Publishing, a division of ABDO, PO Box 398166, Minneapolis, Minnesota 55439.

Printed in the United States of America, North Mankato, Minnesota
102016
012017

THIS BOOK CONTAINS RECYCLED MATERIALS

Interior Photos: Shutterstock Images, 10–11, 23, 45; excerpt from Descender by Jeff Lemire. Copyright 2015 by 171 Studios & Dustin Nguyen., 13, 16, 18, 21; Sergey Novikov/Shutterstock Images, 34–35; © Shannon Watters, Grace Ellis, Noelle Stevenson, & Brooke Allen. All Rights Reserved. Used with Permission., 37, 41; J. Howard Miller/Office for Emergency Management/War Production Board, 38; iStockphoto, 47; Aristotle Saris/AP Images, 56–57, 59, 67; "The Veil," and "The Trip" from PERSEPOLIS: THE STORY OF A CHILDHOOD by Marjane Satrapi, translation copyright © 2003 by L'Association, Paris, France. Used by permission of Pantheon Books, an imprint of the Knopf Doubleday Publishing Group, a division of Penguin Random House LLC. All rights reserved., 61, 63; Everett Historical/Shutterstock Images, 78–79; Graphic Novel Excerpt from THE COMPLETE MAUS: A SURVIVOR'S TALE by Art Spiegelman, Maus, Volume I copyright © 1973, 1980, 1981, 1982, 1983, 1984, 1985, 1986 by Art Spiegelman; Maus, Volume II copyright © 1986, 1989, 1990, 1991 by Art Spiegelman. Used by permission of Pantheon Books, an imprint of the Knopf Doubleday Publishing Group, a division of Penguin Random House LLC. All rights reserved., 81, 83; excerpt from March by John Lewis, Andrew Aydin, and Nate Powell. Copyright 2013. Used by permission of Top Shelf Productions., 87, 89; William A. Smith/AP Images, 91

Editor: Nick Rebman
Series Designer: Maggie Villaume

PUBLISHER'S CATALOGING-IN-PUBLICATION DATA

Names: Dale, Andrew, author.
Title: Graphic novels / by Andrew Dale.
Description: Minneapolis, MN : Abdo Publishing, 2017. | Series: Essential literary genres | Includes bibliographical references and index.
Identifiers: LCCN 2016945204 | ISBN 9781680783797 (lib. bdg.) | ISBN 9781680797329 (ebook)
Subjects: LCSH: Literature--Juvenile literature. | Literary form--Juvenile literature.
Classification: DDC 809--dc23
LC record available at http://lccn.loc.gov/2016945204

CONTENTS

1

INTRODUCTION TO LITERARY GENRES

Why do we read and write literature? Telling stories is an integral part of being human, a universal experience across history and cultures. Literature as we know it today is the written form of these stories and ideas. Writing allows authors to take their readers on a journey that crosses the boundaries of space and time. Literature allows us to understand the experiences of others and express experiences of our own.

What Is a Genre?

A genre is a specific category, or type, of literature. Broad genres of literature include nonfiction, poetry, drama, and fiction. Smaller groupings include subject-based genres such as mystery, science fiction, romance, or fantasy. Literature can also be classified by its audience, such as young adult (YA) or children's, or its format, such as a graphic novel or picture book.

What Are Literary Theory and Criticism?

Literary theory gives us tools to help decode a text. On one level, we can examine the words and phrases the author uses so we can interpret or debate his or her message. We can ask questions about how the book's structure creates an effect on the reader, and whether this is the effect the author intended. We can analyze symbolism or themes in a work. We can dive deeper by asking how a work either supports or challenges society and its values or traditions.

You can look at these questions using different criticisms, or schools of thought. Each type of criticism asks you to look at the work from a different perspective. Perhaps you want to examine what the work says about the writer's life or the time period in which the work was created. Biographical or historical criticism considers these questions. Or perhaps you are interested in what the work says about the role of women or the structure of society. Feminist or Marxist theories seek to answer those types of questions.

How Do You Apply Literary Criticism?

You write an analysis when you use a literary or critical approach to examine and question a work. The theory you choose is a lens through which you can view the work, or a springboard for asking questions about the work. Applying a theory helps you think critically. You are free to question the work and make an assertion about it. If you choose to examine a work using racial criticism, for example, you may ask questions about how the work challenges or upholds racial structures in society. Or you may ask how a character's race affects his or her identity or development throughout the work.

Forming a Thesis

Form your questions and find answers in the work or other related materials. Then you can create a thesis. The thesis is the key point in your analysis. It is your argument about the work based on the school of thought you are using. For example, if you want to approach a work using feminist criticism, you could write the following thesis: The character of Margy in Sissy Johnson's *Margy Sings the Blues* uses her songwriting to subvert traditional gender roles.

HOW TO MAKE A THESIS STATEMENT

In an analysis, a thesis statement typically appears at the end of the introductory paragraph. It is usually only one sentence long and states the author's main idea.

Providing Evidence

Once you have formed a thesis, you must provide evidence to support it. Evidence will usually take the form of examples and quotations from the work itself, often including dialogue from a character. You may wish to address what others have written about the work. Quotes from these individuals may help support your claim. If you find any quotes or examples that contradict your thesis, you will need to create an argument against them. For instance: Many critics claim Margy's actions uphold traditional gender roles, even if her songs went against them. However, the novel's resolution proves Margy had the power to change society through her music.

HOW TO SUPPORT A THESIS STATEMENT

An analysis should include several arguments that support the thesis's claim. An argument is one or two sentences long and is supported by evidence from the work being discussed. Organize the arguments into paragraphs. These paragraphs make up the body of the analysis.

Concluding the Essay

After you have written several arguments and included evidence to support them, finish the essay with a conclusion. The conclusion restates the ideas from the

HOW TO CONCLUDE AN ESSAY

Begin your conclusion with a recap of the thesis and a brief summary of the most important or strongest arguments. Leave readers with a final thought that puts the essay in a larger context or considers its wider implications.

thesis and summarizes some of the main points from the essay. The conclusion's final thought often considers additional implications for the essay or gives the reader something to ponder further.

In This Book

In this book, you will read summaries of works, each followed by an analysis. Critical thinking sections will give you a chance to consider other theses and questions about the work. Did you agree with the author's analysis? What other questions are raised by the thesis and its arguments? You can also see other directions the author could have pursued to analyze the work. Then, in the Analyze It section in the final pages of this book, you will have an opportunity to create your own analysis paper.

Graphic Novels

Graphic novels are a form of literature that evolved out of comics, an art form that uses illustrations and often text to tell a story. Comic strips and monthly comic books typically consist of short stories. Graphic novels distinguish themselves by featuring longer and more intricate narratives. Some monthly comic books are republished in collected editions, and these reformatted versions are also called graphic novels.

Comics are often associated with the superhero genre, which began with the introduction of Superman in 1938. However, comics and graphic novels can focus on any number of topics, including superheroes, mythical monsters, and real historical figures.

Some graphic novels have a single author who is both the writer and the illustrator. Other graphic novels feature multiple contributors: a writer, an illustrator, and one or more other artists such as inkers, colorists, or letterers. Most graphic novels use text in tandem with images to tell the story, but some artists choose to work entirely in pictures.

LOOK FOR THE GUIDES

Throughout the chapters that analyze the works, thesis statements have been highlighted. The box next to the thesis helps explain what questions are being raised about the work. Supporting arguments have also been highlighted. The boxes next to the arguments help explain how these points support the thesis. The conclusions are also accompanied by explanatory boxes. Look for these guides throughout each analysis.

2

AN OVERVIEW OF *DESCENDER: TIN STARS*

Descender: Tin Stars is a graphic novel written by Jeff Lemire and illustrated by Dustin Nguyen. This volume collects the first six issues of the Descender comic book series, which were published from March to August of 2015. The science fiction series is about a young robot who discovers he may be able to help save billions of people across the galaxy from a dangerous new kind of robot called Harvesters.

In the Descender series, the United Galactic Council (UGC) is an alliance of nine planets that have come together to form an interstellar government, similar to the

The United Nations is a global organization dedicated to maintaining world peace.

modern-day United Nations. Humans are one of many different species trying to get along on the futuristic world of Niyrata, the capital planet of the UGC.

Robots in the Skies

Niyrata also has many kinds of advanced technology, including flying cars, spaceships, and robots. From the first few pages of the graphic novel, it is also clear there are almost as many robots as there are people on Niyrata—robots of all shapes and sizes that perform a wide variety of tasks for the citizens of the UGC. These robots appear to be so advanced that they are "people" in their own right, with complex personalities and feelings of their own.

One of Niyrata's inhabitants is Dr. Jin Quon, the man who invented many of the most advanced robots in the galaxy. General Nagoki, the military commander in charge of protecting Niyrata from its enemies, informs Dr. Quon that a giant robot has appeared in the skies above Niyrata. No one on the planet understands what the robot is or where it came from. So far, it has not attempted to communicate with anyone. General Nagoki tells Dr. Quon there are eight more of the giant robots near the other eight planets of the UGC. Because

Dr. Quon is an expert with robotics, the general asks him to learn more about these new and mysterious robots. But before either of them can react, the giant robots' eyes begin to glow a fiery red. General Nagoki and Dr. Quon realize too late that the robots are going to attack. There is a bright flash of light, and the prologue ends.

Prior to the attack, Niyrata is filled with robots that do mundane or dangerous jobs.

A Boy and His Dog

Ten years later, a young boy robot named Tim-21 wakes up on the moon of Dirishu-6, far away from Niyrata and the other core planets of the UGC. Dirishu-6 was a lonely mining colony, and Tim-21 was one of the many robots and people who lived and worked there. But now everyone else seems to be missing.

Tim-21 is happy to be reunited with his robot dog, Bandit. But he is saddened to learn that the people who lived with him on Dirishu-6 died in a horrible accident only a little while after he went to sleep, almost ten years ago. He also finds old news reports about the giant Harvester robots that attacked Niyrata and the other UGC planets. Tim-21 learns that the Harvesters killed millions of people, but almost no robots were killed in the attacks. The people of the UGC became suspicious that their own robots were working with the Harvesters, so the people destroyed almost all of the robots in the galaxy out of fear and revenge.

Tim-21 uses the mining colony's computers to send a distress call, hoping someone will come to his rescue. Then he tries to find out what happened to Andy Tavers and Andy's mother, the humans who were his family on Dirishu-6.

Meanwhile, back on Niyrata, Dr. Quon somehow survived the Harvesters' attack ten years ago. Niyrata is a different place now. Before the Harvesters came, it was bright, clean, and full of people going about their daily lives. Now it looks dirty and run-down, and there are far fewer people living on the planet.

Two officers of the UGC military—a woman named Captain Telsa and a man named Tullis—visit Dr. Quon. Dr. Quon explains that every robot has a built-in code that makes it unique, much like DNA in people. Telsa tells the doctor the UGC has discovered a link between the Harvesters and a robot Dr. Quon created a long time ago: Tim-21. Telsa and Tullis also know Tim-21 is alive, because the UGC received his distress call from Dirishu-6.

Dr. Quon is taken by surprise. He created Tim-21 only to be a companion robot for human children. He thinks it's impossible that there is a connection between Tim-21 and the Harvesters. Telsa, Tullis, and Dr. Quon set out for Dirishu-6 hoping to find Tim-21 and some answers about the deadly Harvesters.

Into the Mining Caves

On Dirishu-6, Tim-21 sees a spaceship landing outside the mining colony. He hopes someone has come to rescue him and Bandit. Instead, the spaceship is full of bounty hunters who want to capture them and sell them for scrap parts. Tim-21 runs deeper into the caves beneath the mining colony. The bounty hunters chase him, and eventually they damage Tim-21 severely using their laser rifles. Suddenly, a huge mining robot called Driller wakes up and helps Tim-21. Driller kills the bounty hunters and tries to figure out how to repair his new friend.

Tim-21 attempts to outrun the bounty hunters.

A flashback scenes shows how Tim-21 first came to Dirishu-6 and met his human family. Dr. Quon created Tim-21 15 years ago and sent him off to the mining colony. Tim-21's job was to be a friend, almost like a brother, to a young human boy named Andy Tavers. Tim-21 and Andy eventually came to like each other, and Tim-21 started calling Andy's mother Mommy.

After the bounty hunters damage Tim-21, he has a strange dream in which he meets other robots that were destroyed by their former masters after the Harvesters attacked. These robots tell Tim-21 their former masters turned on them, becoming cruel because they feared the Harvesters. The robots beg Tim-21 to find them and free them from their purgatory-like state in Tim-21's dream.

The Melting Pits

Telsa, Tullis, and Dr. Quon arrive on Dirishu-6 to find Driller carrying Tim-21 out of the mining caves. Dr. Quon takes Tim-21 into the spaceship and tries to repair him. Tim-21 wakes up and tells the doctor and the others about his strange dream. With all of the people and robots now aboard the spacecraft, Telsa and Tullis set a course back to Niyrata. In a private conversation, Telsa informs Dr. Quon she wants to use Tim-21 to find out how to defeat the Harvesters if they ever return. What she doesn't tell him is that her mother was killed by the Harvesters when she was very young.

Suddenly, another spaceship appears. This new ship is carrying more bounty hunters. They have been hired by the planet Gnish, home of a warlike people who suffered greatly when the Harvesters attacked. The Gnishians want to eliminate all robots in the galaxy and will pay anyone who brings robots to their home planet. Once there, the robots will be tossed into the Melting

Dr. Quon repairs Tim-21 as Tullis and Telsa look on.

Pits, a gladiator-style fighting arena where robots are forced to battle each other to the death.

Tim-21, Bandit, Driller, Telsa, Tullis, and Dr. Quon are all captured and taken to Gnish. There they meet King S'nok III, a cruel Gnishian who throws Driller, Bandit, and Tullis (even though he's human) into the Melting Pits. While the others fight for their lives against other robots, S'nok interrogates Dr. Quon about Tim-21 and his connection to the Harvesters.

Meanwhile, on Niyrata, General Nagoki (who also survived the Harvester attacks) discusses the UGC's discovery of Tim-21 with members of the government. When Nagoki mentions his plans for Tim-21, the other council members realize he wants to use the information inside Tim-21 to create his own army of robots in case the Harvesters ever return. None of the people in the room, including Nagoki, are aware that one of Nagoki's assistants is actually a robot. This assistant is an agent of a secret robot organization called the Hardwire—a group of rebel robots who are fighting back against antirobot violence in the galaxy—and she has been sent to discover Tim-21's whereabouts. When she overhears that Tim-21 and his friends are on Gnish, she radios this information to the Hardwire and then self-destructs.

Dr. Quon's Secret

While being tortured by King S'nok, Dr. Quon reveals he did not invent all of his robots. Fifteen years ago—before building Tim-21 and the other robots, and before the Harvesters came—Dr. Quon and his professor, Solomon, journeyed to a distant planet called Ostrakon. On this planet, buried among the ruins of an ancient civilization, Dr. Quon and Solomon found a single robot that was more advanced than anything they had ever seen before. They brought back the robot to their spaceship. The ancient robot woke up shouting about mysterious persecutors who would come to do everyone harm. Concerned for their safety, Solomon shut down the robot.

Against Solomon's wishes, Dr. Quon secretly stole the advanced technology from this robot's brain and used it to build his own new robots, including Tim-21. Dr. Quon became famous across all the planets of the UGC for his genius in creating such incredible technologies.

As Dr. Quon finishes his story, Telsa realizes Dr. Quon's theft may have somehow led to the Harvester attacks ten years ago. King S'nok decides to kill Dr. Quon because he doesn't actually know anything

Psius rescues Tim-21 and his friends from the Gnishians.

useful about Tim-21. But before S'nok can order the execution, an explosion blows a hole in the wall.

Several robots with laser rifles march in. Their leader, Psius, declares he and his group are the Hardwire and have come for Tim-21. They quickly take the Gnishians prisoner and free Tim-21, Telsa, and Dr. Quon. Psius then introduces Tim-21 to a small robot whom Psius refers to as his son—a robot called Tim-22.

3

WORKING-CLASS HEROES

Science fiction has a long history of imagining futuristic societies that feature a wide variety of alien cultures and technologically advanced robots. Sometimes these great societies of the future have solved many of humanity's modern problems, such as poverty, racism, and inequality. The society in the Descender series has solved problems but for only some of its people. Descender imagines a world in which life is good for people—that is, humans and their alien allies. However, for the robots throughout the galaxy, life is much more difficult. The robots exist for only one reason: to provide labor. The robots are denied any opportunity to improve their lives or follow their own desires.

Throughout history, people have lived under similar circumstances. This has often led observers to ask

Science fiction stories are often set in densely populated cities filled with highly advanced technology.

questions about their society's class structures. Who are the people who do most of the work in a society, and for whom do they work? Are the people of the working class allowed to share in the benefits of their labor? Is there also a ruling class that believes most or all of the society's wealth and opportunities belong only to the rich and powerful?

Marxist criticism examines how a person's social status affects his or her access to wealth. It also investigates how a society's laws or unwritten rules can keep certain people from improving their lives and their well-being. Marxist criticism can also explain the political revolutions that sometimes occur when a society continues to oppress a certain group of people over a long period of time. As the primary laborers of a disadvantaged social group in their society, the robots of Descender are a representation of the working class being pushed toward violent revolution.

THESIS STATEMENT

The thesis statement outlines the main argument for the essay: "As the primary laborers of a disadvantaged social group in their society, the robots of Descender are a representation of the working class being pushed toward violent revolution."

The robots in Descender perform almost all of the most basic labor in their society, which is a hallmark of the working class; meanwhile, people hold all the positions of wealth and power, which is a key characteristic of the ruling class. On the earliest pages of the first chapter, robots can be seen in the background carrying out a wide variety of tasks. They are nannies, personal assistants, bodyguards, and pilots. Some of these tasks may be difficult or dangerous, but they do not usually come with much recognition or prestige. Robots do the jobs that make society run smoothly, but they get little reward or thanks for performing these jobs. Nonrobots, on the other hand, make all of the important decisions for the United Galactic Council, and they hold many positions of wealth and power. They are doctors, inventors, military commanders, and business leaders. These drastic differences between the positions robots and nonrobots hold in their society highlight the social classes to which they belong.

ARGUMENT ONE

The author's first argument examines how the society is organized: "The robots in Descender perform almost all of the most basic labor in their society, which is a hallmark of the working class; meanwhile, people hold all the positions of wealth and power, which is a key characteristic of the ruling class."

Driller, the mining robot on Dirishu-6, is an example of a working-class robot. His job is simple, and it requires very little skill or education. But he must do it day in and day out, or else the society will run out of resources. His name, Driller, gives the impression that he does not have an identity of his own and that his value as an individual does not extend beyond his job. Once that job no longer exists, he seems lost and confused as he tries to figure out where to go and what to do next. The UGC does not even bother to send anyone to rescue the robots such as Driller, who were stranded on Dirishu-6 after their human masters died. The people of the UGC apparently think of robots as disposable and replaceable. This is often the case in societies with strict social classes; working-class citizens are left to fend for themselves, while the rest of the society benefits from the work they have done.

Dr. Quon, a member of the ruling class, is an example of a powerful and influential human in the galaxy. As the supposed inventor of many of the most advanced robot technologies, other people (and even some robots) look up to him and respect him. He lives in a beautiful, spacious apartment on Niyrata, the capital planet of the UGC, and he appears to have at least one robot servant. When the Harvesters attack, it is Dr. Quon who General Nagoki calls for help. This suggests Dr. Quon has a strong relationship with the galaxy's military forces. In the sixth chapter, Dr. Quon reveals he stole all of his amazing inventions, meaning he has not done much to contribute to the society that has given him wealth and power. This situation stands in stark contrast to robots such as Driller, who work hard every day of their lives and receive almost nothing in return.

The robots in Descender also have fewer rights and less power to make decisions, placing them in a lower social class than the UGC's nonrobot citizens. At some point in history, the UGC decided robots would be people's servants. None of the people in the story seem to give any thought to what the robots might want. In fact, Descender's story revolves around what other people want from Tim-21, not what he wants for himself. Captain Telsa only pretends to help him find Andy and his mother. In truth, all she wants from

ARGUMENT TWO

The author's second argument points out the oppression robots experience because of their social class: "The robots in Descender also have fewer rights and less power to make decisions, placing them in a lower social class than the UGC's nonrobot citizens."

Tim-21 is to find out how to fight the Harvesters if they ever return to attack the UGC planets. General Nagoki seeks something similar, while the Gnishians merely want to destroy all robots, buying them and throwing them into their gladiator pits as cheap, disposable entertainment. Even Dr. Quon, who is perhaps the friendliest person toward Tim-21, seems to be interested in him only as an experiment rather than as an individual with his own desires and feelings.

Most robots accept these circumstances without protesting or fighting back against their oppressors. But the Harvesters provide an example of what happens when a robot acts outside the narrow roles that people have defined for them. The society is shaken to its core, and people can no longer live lives of luxury at the expense of their robot servants. The people blame all robots for the attacks rather than blaming only those that were responsible. This attitude sparks a kind of class warfare in which the ruling class punishes the entire working class for the actions of a few robots who dared to upset the social order. Though the Harvesters' actual motives are still unclear, the nonrobot citizens of the UGC believe themselves superior to robots, causing them to overreact against all robots.

This violence and persecution leads some robots to seek revolution, another key characteristic of an oppressed working class according to Marxist criticism. In the fifth and sixth chapters of *Descender: Tin Stars*, it becomes clear that many of the robots were unhappy with how people treated them, even before the Harvester attack. Some of the robots have created a resistance group, calling themselves the Hardwire. They wish to start a revolution and build a new society in which robots are treated fairly. The Hardwire has secretly infiltrated the UGC because robots have no voice in galactic politics. Group members resort to violence both to defend themselves and because they believe the revolution must be started by force.

ARGUMENT THREE

In the third argument, the author describes the revolutionary reactions that often arise from an oppressed working class: "This violence and persecution leads some robots to seek revolution, another key characteristic of an oppressed working class according to Marxist criticism."

In contrast to the people, who treat robots as second-class citizens, the robots of the Hardwire treat other robots as equals. For example, Psius, the leader of the resistance, refers to Tim-21 as *he* instead of *it*, showing he believes Tim-21 is a person rather than a member of a lower class or an object to be mistreated.

Psius seems to genuinely care about Tim-21's well-being. He and the rest of the rebels have taken great risks to find Tim-21—something the people were willing to do only after they discovered Tim-21 had something valuable they wanted. The robotic revolutionaries of the Hardwire exemplify the ideals of a more equal society, in which social class would not be a barrier holding citizens back.

Similar to many science fiction stories, Descender uses an imaginary future to ask questions about how people organize their societies and who benefits the most and the least from hierarchical systems such as social class. The robots in Descender provide the basic goods and services in their society but do not receive any of the benefits of their labor. After suffering years of oppression at the hands of their nonrobot masters, they decide to reject the society's class structures and embrace a revolution, reflecting some of the most common patterns and characteristics of the working class according to Marxist literary theory.

CONCLUSION

The final paragraph summarizes the author's thesis and restates the three arguments that support it.

THINKING CRITICALLY

Now it's your turn to assess the essay. Consider these questions:

1. Can you find any evidence in Descender that disproves the author's thesis?
2. Do you see any parallels between the plight of the robots in Descender and people who live in real-world societies with strict class structures?
3. Marxist criticism addresses the economic stratification of a society, but a person's social class is often influenced by facets of his or her identity. How might a Marxist reading of Descender be combined with criticisms from other perspectives, such as race or gender?

OTHER APPROACHES

The previous essay, which examines *Descender: Tin Stars* from a Marxist point of view, is only one way to examine this graphic novel. Another approach might choose to explore the racial tensions between humans and robots, while still another approach might be interested in the historical context from which Descender arises.

Critical Race Theory

The robots in Descender experience violence and systematic oppression at the hands of their nonrobot masters because robots are outwardly different from people. This could be seen as a metaphor for the ways in which real people have treated each other based on superficial characteristics such as physical appearance or place of origin. A thesis from the perspective of critical race theory could be: The people in Descender hold stereotypical beliefs and suspicions about robots, and this leads to racism and persecution that mirrors the experiences of many racial and ethnic groups in the real world.

New Historicism

New historicism attempts to understand a work by considering the key concerns and ideas of the time period during which the work was created. Descender was written in the 2010s in North America, a time and place where high technology was unavoidable in everyday life and extremely intelligent computers were becoming more and more common. A thesis written from a new historicist approach could be: Descender's attempt to humanize a race of robots reflects modern uncertainties about technology and the increasingly powerful role it plays in daily life.

4

AN OVERVIEW OF *LUMBERJANES: BEWARE THE KITTEN HOLY*

Lumberjanes: Beware the Kitten Holy, written by Noelle Stevenson and Grace Ellis and illustrated by Brooke Allen, is a collected edition of the first four issues of the Lumberjanes comic book series. The graphic novel, published in 2015, is set at a girls' summer camp where the campers are known as Lumberjanes. Five of the Lumberjanes—teenagers named April, Mal, Molly, Jo, and Ripley—share Roanoke Cabin under the watchful eye of their camp counselor, Jen. The girls encounter increasingly strange

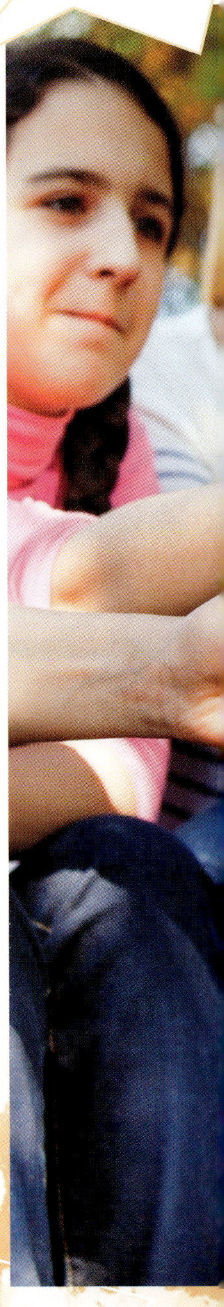

Beware the Kitten Holy adds elements of supernatural mystery to a story about a summer camp.

adventures and monsters in the wilderness outside the campground, and they begin to unravel a mystery involving the "kitten holy."

Creatures in the Forest

The graphic novel opens with April walking through the woods alone at night. April, who appears to be dressed as Little Red Riding Hood, is startled when her friends Mal and Molly sneak up behind her. April and the other girls from Roanoke Cabin are following a mysterious woman who appeared in their campground and went off into the woods. Soon their friend Jo joins them as well, and they hear a howling noise.

Suddenly the girls are attacked by a group of three-eyed foxes. April, Mal, Molly, and Jo attempt to fight off the foxes together. Soon Ripley, the fifth Roanoke girl, joins the fray. She pummels a fox with her fists. The fox disappears into thin air, and a strange golden ring drops to the ground beneath it. The other foxes all howl a warning: "Beware the kitten holy."[1]

The Lumberjanes are bewildered. Jo picks up the golden ring, while the other girls debate what just happened. They have no idea where the foxes came from, nor what "Beware the kitten holy" means. In the

Each of the Lumberjanes has a distinct personality.

end, they decide to get back to Roanoke Cabin before Jen wakes up. The girls try to sneak back into bed unnoticed, but Jen turns on the cabin lights. She was waiting for the girls to return.

Rosie the Camp Director

Jen is angry with her campers, so she takes them to Rosie, the camp director. Jen informs Rosie of all the rules the girls broke. Rosie—who bears a striking resemblance to Rosie the Riveter, a fictional icon from the days of World War II (1939–1945)—clearly enjoys chopping wood, because she has an ax and a log on her desk. Rosie asks to hear the girls' side of the story.

After Jo and April finish telling the story, Molly nervously asks Rosie if she is going to call their parents. Instead of answering the question, Rosie asks the girls if they know the Lumberjanes pledge. All five girls know the pledge by heart: they promise to be good friends, respect nature, and make the world a better place for everyone. When the girls have finished the pledge, Rosie tells them they will see strange things at camp this summer, but they should stick together and help each other no matter what.

Rosie the Riveter was a character who encouraged women to work in factories while men were fighting in World War II.

Monsters in the Water

The next day, Jen prepares the girls for a canoe trip. The six young women set out on the river in their three canoes. Dangerous rapids appear downriver, and Jen shouts for everyone to paddle to shore. April and Jo are in the lead, and they get caught by the swift river currents. Molly decides to rescue them, and she paddles furiously to catch up while Mal hangs on for dear life. Ripley plays the reckless heroine again, leaping from her canoe and swimming toward Molly and Mal. Molly and Mal pull Ripley into their canoe before she is swept away by the rapids.

Suddenly, a giant three-eyed eel monster bursts from the water ahead of the campers. It slams one of its tentacles into Molly and Mal's canoe. Mal is thrown overboard. Molly dives in after her. The monster picks up April and Jo's canoe with another tentacle, terrifying the campers. April pulls a scrunchie from her hair and snaps it from her fingers into the monster's eyes. The monster tosses April and Jo's canoe into the air and dives back under the water, leaving the campers to swim desperately toward shore.

Molly wades out of the river carrying Mal, who isn't breathing. As Molly, April, and Jo try to remember how to perform CPR, Ripley takes a running start and leaps onto Mal's stomach. Mal spits up all the water on which she had been choking. Reunited on the shore (minus Jen, who managed to keep clear of the rapids in her canoe), the five Lumberjanes try to figure out how to get back to camp before dark. They head off into the woods.

Secrets in the Woods

A while later, Ripley complains that she's hungry and pulls a candy bar from her pocket. As she unwraps it, an eagle swoops down from the sky and snatches it from Ripley's hands. Ripley scrambles to the top of a tree, hoping to catch the eagle. Just as it flies beyond her reach, Ripley spots something in the distance: a tower standing on the edge of a cliff above a lake.

As Ripley climbs down, she trips on a branch. It turns out to be a secret lever that opens a trapdoor at the base of the tree. The others aren't sure about venturing into the cave, but Ripley leaps headfirst down the hole. Her friends have no choice but to jump in after her. The Lumberjanes find themselves in an ancient-looking temple full of statues.

The girls venture farther into the underground tunnels. Eventually they come to a large cavern where a giant Hercules-like statue awaits them. The statue wakes up and demands that one of the Lumberjanes arm-wrestle him for the privilege of passing through the magic doorway he guards. April accepts the challenge. She and the statue begin the arm-wrestling match, and for a few moments they struggle mightily. But April is a champion arm-wrestler, and she snaps the statue's stone arm off of his shoulder. The magical door creaks open, and the stunned statue stands aside.

The girls discover an underground chamber filled with statues.

Traps in the Caverns

Farther down the tunnel, Molly sets off a booby trap that shoots dozens of arrows out of the walls. The girls run for their lives, and just when they've made it out of the hallway of arrows, Molly accidentally awakens another living statue. This one is shaped like a man but has the head of an owl and a glowing gem at the center of its chest. Mal notices the gem's shape perfectly matches a keyhole in the door ahead of them, so she and Ripley tackle the statue. Mal grabs the gem from its chest and fits it into the keyhole in the door. The Lumberjanes hurry through the doorway and slam it shut behind them.

The girls find a brightly illuminated wall inscribed with strange phrases, including "beware the kitten holy." Molly realizes the phrases must be anagrams. She jumbles up the letters and comes up with "in the tower by the lake"—just like the one Ripley saw when she climbed the tree. The Lumberjanes decide to check out the tower, so they leave the caverns and return to camp.

In the Tower by the Lake

The next day, Jen takes the Lumberjanes on a hike through the woods. While searching for rare plants, they stumble upon a yeti. Jen and the girls flee through the forest, tumbling down a hill and landing in poison ivy. They are discovered by a troop of Scouting Lads from the nearby boys' camp. The boys invite the girls back to their camp, where they offer the girls tea and cookies.

As the girls enjoy their refreshments, the boys' hypermasculine camp director bursts into the cabin. He is furious that the boys have invited girls into their campground. He criticizes the boys for baking cookies and serving tea, which he thinks is unmanly.

The Lumberjanes convince some of the boys to distract Jen while they sneak out of the camp to look for the tower by the lake. The tower is close to the boys' camp, but the girls find it guarded by yetis. Luckily, Ripley pocketed most of the cookies from the boys' cabin, and she bribes the yetis to let them into the tower. At the top of the tower, the Lumberjanes find a magical bow and some arrows, which they decide to borrow until they've solved all of the forest's mysteries.

Magic Spells and Mind Control

Meanwhile, back at the boys' camp, Jen notices that her campers have left her behind. But before she can run out into the woods to search for them, all of the boys seem to fall under a magic spell. Their eyes turn blank, and they begin foaming at the mouth. Jen is terrified as the boys chase her out of the camp. As she flees, she runs into her campers, and they all run across a rope bridge over a deep gorge. Molly, who has earned her Robyn Hood badge, uses the bow and arrow to shoot the ropes. The bridge collapses into the gorge below, and the Scouting Lads are stuck on the other side. Jen apologizes to the Lumberjanes for not believing in the monsters. The girls accept her apology. They decide to solve the mysteries together from now on.

The graphic novel ends on a cliffhanger. The Scouting Lads are still under the magic spell. A shadowy figure, who looks suspiciously similar to the hypermasculine camp director, scolds them for allowing the girls to escape. But the shadowy man grins and says, "YOU HAVE FAILED ME—but don't worry lads. Next time, we'll be prepared."[2]

The Lumberjanes have many skills that are not traditionally associated with girls, including archery.

5

DIVERSE GENDER IDENTITIES

Gender studies is a form of literary criticism that examines how a society's concepts of gender are constructed, and it questions the traditional binary between male and female. Gender studies includes ideas of gender being flexible from person to person and constantly changing throughout a society. *Beware the Kitten Holy* argues that its heroines' diverse and nontraditional gender identities allow them to face a wide variety of challenges and remain strong in the face of adversity.

THESIS STATEMENT

The thesis statement outlines the main argument for the essay: "*Beware the Kitten Holy* argues that its heroines' diverse and nontraditional gender identities allow them to face a wide variety of challenges and remain strong in the face of adversity."

Although April looks similar to Little Red Riding Hood in the opening scene, she is not helpless.

ARGUMENT ONE

The first argument discusses some ways gender traditionally has been constructed and how the main characters defy it: "*Beware the Kitten Holy* challenges common stereotypes about masculine and feminine gender identities by featuring heroines who come from all over the spectrum of gender."

Beware the Kitten Holy challenges common stereotypes about masculine and feminine gender identities by featuring heroines who come from all over the spectrum of gender. The graphic novel first introduces April, the character whose gender identity is perhaps the most traditionally feminine. Her outward appearance suggests she fits many stereotypes of a teenage girl. However, April quickly proves she can hold her own in a brawl with magical foxes, in a canoe on dangerous rapids, and in an arm-wrestling match.

April combines a wide variety of interests and skills into a single personality, defying both traditional male and female roles. Lumberjanes uses similar techniques in creating its other main characters. Molly and Mal think spiders are gross, but Molly is talented at canoeing and archery, while Mal displays impressive physical strength. Jo is good at math and often serves as the calm, rational thinker of the group. Ripley is an animal lover who brings curiosity and courage to the group in moments of uncertainty. None of the Roanoke girls conforms to any strict constructions of gender. Instead, they pursue different talents and interests, making each of them a unique and well-rounded character. When the five of them come together, this variety of personalities, skills, and experiences means they are well equipped to deal with the mysteries and dangers they encounter.

The camp director, Rosie, also has traits that traditionally have been considered masculine, which affirms her campers' pursuit of skills and interests that might otherwise be off-limits because of their gender. Rosie's office shows she enjoys chopping lumber with an ax and carving sculptures out of wood. As the director of a scouting camp for girls, she is likely an expert in the same skills her campers use to navigate the wilderness. The name *Lumberjanes* itself is a play on the word *lumberjack*, a job traditionally performed by men. The Lumberjanes

ARGUMENT TWO

The second argument cites one of the main characters' role models from whom they learn how to navigate their own gender identities: "The camp director, Rosie, also has traits that traditionally have been considered masculine, which affirms her campers' pursuit of skills or interests that might otherwise be off-limits because of their gender."

respect Rosie's authority, but they also trust the advice she offers them and look up to her as a role model.

Rosie's appearance, too, supports her campers' pursuit of their skills and interests regardless of gender. She is clearly based on Rosie the Riveter, a well-known fictional icon of American women who took on a variety of traditionally male-occupied jobs during World War II. Rosie the Riveter has a can-do attitude, which Rosie the camp director reflects to her campers. She is an example of a woman who has broken into male-dominated areas of American culture and found she can be successful. By serving as a positive, encouraging role model who challenges expectations of gender roles, Rosie creates a safe space for her campers to explore the talents that will help them through their adventures at summer camp.

The Scouting Lads support the graphic novel's argument for diverse, nontraditional gender roles by providing an example of the opposite—they conform to one strict gender

ARGUMENT THREE

The third argument discusses an opposite example of gender roles that supports the thesis: "The Scouting Lads support the graphic novel's argument for diverse, nontraditional gender roles by providing an example of the opposite—they conform to one strict gender role that denies them the freedom and adaptability the Lumberjanes enjoy."

role that denies them the freedom and adaptability the Lumberjanes enjoy. At first the Scouting Lads seem similar to the Lumberjanes. In some ways they also defy gender roles: they enjoy baking, serving tea and cookies, and keeping their cabins clean. All of these hobbies and tasks were traditionally assigned to women in American culture. However, as soon as the Scouting Lads fall under the magic spell, the boys all conform to a single identity.

The magic spell forces the Scouting Lads to take on a narrow set of behaviors. They all share the same goal: to capture Jen. While they have strength in numbers, the Scouting Lads do not have the same variety of skills as the Lumberjanes. They cannot adapt to new situations or think on their feet. Molly's creative thinking and archery skills trap the Scouting Lads on the opposite side of the gorge, allowing the Lumberjanes to escape. Under the magic spell, the Scouting Lads have no such skills or quick thinking to help them succeed.

Further, the shadowy figure controlling the Scouting Lads is almost certainly their camp director, who believes males should all conform to the traditional ideal of the gender. His mind-control spell forces the boys to behave in a hypermasculine way and attack the

Lumberjanes; essentially, the spell turns the boys into monsters who cannot think for themselves. In contrast, the boys are much kinder and more intelligent when they are free to create their own identities.

Lumberjanes uses its whole cast of characters to argue that a diversity of gender identities leads to a stronger, more adaptable society. It offers a wide variety of perspectives that support this argument, including the Scouting Lads, who are forced to obey traditional gender roles; Rosie, a woman who chooses skills and roles that traditionally belonged to men; and the Lumberjanes, a group of girls who create a strong, versatile community with many hobbies and interests from all over the spectrum of gender. In these ways, *Lumberjanes* accurately reflects ways in which Americans negotiate and define their own gender identities.

CONCLUSION

The last paragraph concludes the argument by restating the thesis and arguments. It comes back to the benefits of diversity of gender identities and shows how the graphic novel supports this idea.

THINKING CRITICALLY

Now it's your turn to assess the essay. Consider these questions:

1. Can you find evidence in Lumberjanes that disproves the author's thesis?
2. Gender studies also explores the role of oppression in a society's traditional ideals of gender. Are there characters in Lumberjanes who are marginalized because of their gender identity? If so, what are the consequences?
3. American constructions of gender have changed radically over time. The teenage Lumberjanes and Scouting Lads hold beliefs on gender that are different from those of the boys' camp director, who is much older than the campers. Do you see any parallels between the conflict between generations in Lumberjanes and discussions of gender issues in the real world?

OTHER APPROACHES

The previous essay is only one example of how to analyze the graphic novel Lumberjanes. Another approach might focus on the graphic novel's depiction of the natural world. Yet another option is to examine the story from a feminist perspective.

Ecocriticism

Much of the action in Lumberjanes takes place outdoors, in forests, rivers, and mysterious underground caverns. These locations are often full of dangerous monsters that usually resemble real animals, and the Lumberjanes must overcome these creatures before they can proceed to the next stage of their adventure. Ecocriticism asks how a text portrays the relationship between humans and nature. A thesis from an ecocritic's perspective might be: Though Lumberjanes is about a summer camp for girls who love nature, the graphic novel actually depicts the natural world as untamed and dangerous, something to be feared and avoided rather than loved, understood, or cared for.

Feminist Criticism

Lumberjanes presents a close-knit group of young women who find themselves up against a belligerent, domineering camp director and his army of mind-controlled boy scouts. The camp director is an extreme stereotype of traditional masculinity, imposing his opinions about men and women on both his campers and the Lumberjanes. Feminist criticism examines how patriarchy (a male-dominated society) oppresses women and raises men who participate in that oppression. A feminist criticism of this graphic novel could be: The Lumberjanes are a diverse group of women coming together to reject the patriarchy represented by the boys' camp director and unwillingly supported by the Scouting Lads under his influence.

6

AN OVERVIEW OF *PERSEPOLIS*

Persepolis: The Story of a Childhood, originally published in 2000, is a graphic novel written and illustrated by Marjane Satrapi. It is an autobiographical story about growing up in Iran from the mid-1970s through the early 1980s. Iran experienced widespread social and economic turmoil during this period. Groups such as Marxists and Islamic fundamentalists demonstrated against the shah, the king of the nation. In *Persepolis*, Satrapi uses her childhood in Iran and her relationships with her family to tell a broader story about her country, which she believes is largely misunderstood by Western cultures.

Iranian citizens took part in protests against the shah in 1978.

God, Marx, and the Shah of Iran

Satrapi begins the graphic novel in the years leading up to the Islamic Revolution of 1979. Known to her friends and family as Marji, she becomes interested in politics at a young age through listening to her parents talk about demonstrations. Marji learns about Marxism and the socialist revolutionaries of Iran from books her parents give to her. Marji is also a religious girl who enjoys private conversations with God after she has gone to bed for the night. When her schoolteacher asks Marji what she wants to be when she grows up, Marji replies, "I'll be a prophet."[1] Her reasons for wanting to be a prophet are simple: she wishes all people could be treated as equals and that no one should have to suffer.

Her faith in God is matched only by her fascination with politics and revolution. When Marji and her friends get together to play, they pretend to be famous revolutionaries such as Fidel Castro, Che Guevara, and Leon Trotsky. Dressed up as their Communist heroes, the children hold mock demonstrations in the garden at the Satrapi home. But after the shah's police burn down a theater with 400 people locked inside, Marji decides to go with her parents and join the real protests in the streets. Her parents fear for Marji's safety, so they tell her she can participate when she gets older.

Never one to give in, Marji declares that she loves the shah because he was chosen by God. Her parents, Ebi and Taji, seem surprised, but Ebi tries to clarify the situation for his daughter. He explains that the emperor of Iran (to whom Marji is related) was overthrown when a military officer named Reza Khan led a small group that seized control of the country. But Reza had help from the British, who wanted access to Iran's large reserves of oil. Ebi, Taji, and other Iranians dislike the foreign influence of the United Kingdom and the United

Anti-government protests brought many Iranians out into the streets in 1978.

States. They organize protests against the current shah, who is Reza's son.

As Marji grows older, she recognizes things about her own life that make her appreciate her parents' Marxist political views. She reads books about poverty among many Iranians, and for the first time Marji realizes why she feels ashamed to ride in her father's Cadillac. She feels guilty about being wealthy while others have little or no money. She also feels compassion for her family's maid, Mehri, with whom she has always had a close, almost sisterlike bond. This connection with Mehri leads Marji to decide she favors the revolution. Together, Marji and Mehri attend their first demonstration against the shah.

The Islamic Revolution

One day, the revolution finally does come. But the result is not what Marji or her parents were hoping for. People celebrate in the streets when the shah from Iran, and Ebi and Taji's friends return home after years in prison. But instead of a new government that embraces Ebi and Taji's Marxist ideals, a theocracy comes to power. A theocracy is a government based upon a specific religion—in this case, Islam. Though Marji and her parents are Muslims,

Marji and her friends do not understand the purpose of their veils, so they use them as toys.

they do not hold the same fundamentalist beliefs as the country's new rulers. Once again, they are political outsiders, just as they were when the shah was in power.

Marji begins to notice the changes around her almost immediately. Her school closes for a while. When it reopens, girls and boys are separated. Each girl must wear a hijab, a veil that covers a woman's head, neck, shoulders, and chest. Men are required to wear loose clothing and must not shave their beards. Soon Marji hears about the government murdering people for their political beliefs, and some of her friends and family leave the country to escape the new Islamic regime.

Uncle Anoosh

During this time, Marji gets to know her uncle Anoosh, who was imprisoned by the shah but released after the revolution. Marji adores Anoosh. He tells her stories of his time in prison. He also speaks about his life in Russia, where he got married and had two children. He believes the Islamic leaders don't understand how to govern and will eventually leave the rule of Iran to the people. But the religious rulers do not leave. They continue finding new ways to control the Iranian people and oppress those who disagree with their fundamentalist beliefs.

As time goes on, Marji, Ebi, Taji, and Anoosh (who now lives with the Satrapi family) watch more of their friends disappear or die at the hands of the government. Many more of their acquaintances leave Iran to avoid such a fate. Ebi and Taji also discuss going to the United States, but they are too attached to their country and their lifestyle as wealthy citizens. They both realize the Islamic regime is rounding up all of the revolutionaries who once opposed the shah, but they decide to stay in Iran anyway.

One day Anoosh is taken back to prison. He is allowed to have one visitor, and he requests Marji. In his prison cell, he encourages Marji to be hopeful. Marji doesn't seem to understand, but this is the last time she will see him alive. Soon after, the government executes Anoosh for being a Russian spy. Marji is devastated.

Weeping in her bed one night, God visits her again. Marji is furious with God, telling him to get out of her life. She feels more lost and alone than ever.

The War with Iraq

Over the next few years, Marji's relationships with her parents and with her country become even more complicated. Though she mistrusts Iran's government and hates it for killing Anoosh, she is also patriotic. When the neighboring country of Iraq attacks Iran, Marji and her father bond over their shared anger at the Iraqis. During the war, the Satrapi family deals with shortages of goods, including food and gasoline. The government closes all of Iran's universities because they are symbols of imperialism—that is,

Marji and her family struggle to adjust to the new government's rules.

symbols of the Western countries that supported the shah's government.

The war with Iraq also brings to light an even uglier side of Iran's Islamic government, as the police begin rounding up political opponents and executing them. Iran's leaders also use the Iranian casualties of war to drum up support among the people. Marji and her schoolmates are forced to participate in the ritual of beating their breasts to honor the country's fallen soldiers. Marji and her friends think these rituals are silly, openly mocking them in front of their teachers. But they also begin to realize the war has real consequences. From the family's new maid, Mrs. Nasrine, Marji learns the government indoctrinates young boys to fight for Iran. She fears her friends will be sent to war.

A Rebellious Teenager

Similar to many teenagers, Marji also experiences conflict with her parents. Though she still loves them, Marji finds their rules frustrating. Marji embraces hobbies and symbols of the West, especially of the United Kingdom and the United States. She starts smoking, and she likes to wear a denim jacket covered in buttons and pins featuring the names of her favorite musicians. One day Marji goes out to buy music tapes, which are forbidden. On her way home, she is stopped and questioned by Iran's secret police. Marji lies to them and manages to escape with her tapes, but she doesn't tell her mother what happened because she fears never being allowed to leave the house again.

Eventually, Ebi and Taji decide Iran has become too dangerous for Marji. They know she will never cooperate with the government's religious laws or practices. So Marji's parents find a way to send her to a French school in Austria, where she can continue to learn, express her personality, and enjoy her hobbies. Marji quickly realizes her parents will not be going to Austria with her.

Marji invites her friends over and gives away many of her most prized possessions. She spends one last night in her parents' home and says good-bye to her grandmother the next morning. At the airport, Marji's sadness seems to outweigh her excitement about the independence that awaits her. The graphic novel ends with Marji leaving her parents behind, beginning a new stage of her life in a foreign country.

7

POSTCOLONIAL IDENTITY

Persepolis tells the story of a girl's coming of age during an especially tumultuous time in her country. She is caught between war, revolution, and religious fervor. But the graphic novel is also the story of a nation struggling to find a new identity separate from the influences of the United Kingdom and the United States, both of which took advantage of political turmoil in Iran during the 1900s for their own ends.

Though Iran was never colonized by the United Kingdom or the United States, the countries occupied Iran during World War II, and the repeated Anglo-American interference in Iran's politics has changed the course of the nation's history. Postcolonial criticism examines how powerful nations have conquered, controlled, and oppressed the people

Riots in the late 1970s were the result of political and religious turmoil in Iran.

of other nations. Postcolonialism also studies the aftermath of this oppression—how people recover and reform their identities, both personal and national, after they have broken free of colonialism. *Persepolis* is one author's take on this process. Marji represents a postcolonial identity that blends the cultures of both the colonizers and the colonized, and her new cultural identity is complicated, compassionate, and often conflicts with the reactionary Islamic regime.

THESIS STATEMENT

The thesis statement outlines the main argument for the essay: "Marji represents a postcolonial identity that blends the cultures of both the colonizers and the colonized, and her new cultural identity is complicated, compassionate, and often conflicts with the reactionary Islamic regime."

Throughout the graphic novel, Marji describes her family's strong cultural and political ties to Iran, and she carries forward this history of social activism as part of a new generation of postcolonial Iranians. The rich culture of Iran that Marji values so highly is

ARGUMENT ONE

The author's first argument describes Marji's native Iranian culture and how she chooses to embody it: "Throughout the graphic novel, Marji describes her family's strong cultural and political ties to Iran, and she carries forward this history of social activism as part of a new generation of postcolonial Iranians."

multifaceted, tying together religion, history, family, and politics. Early on, Marji says, "I was born with religion. At the age of six, I was already sure I was the last prophet."[1] She also has "big discussions" with God about her path to becoming a prophet.[2] Satrapi uses her six-year-old imagination to show her fascination with Iran's religious background. Marji's faith remains a strong part of her personality throughout her childhood, but it shares an equal space with her interest in Marxism.

As Iran heads toward revolution, inspired partly by Marxists such as Marji's parents, Marji takes an interest in the revolutionary figures who fought against the shah's rule. By extension, these figures also fought against the imperialist plans of the United Kingdom and the United States. When Marji learns about Karl Marx and his political ideas, she says, "It was funny to see how much Marx and God looked like each other."[3] God and Marx are both figures that have had tremendous influence on Iran's culture and politics. They offer Marji two unique but intersecting ways to understand her identity as a postcolonial Iranian.

Marji's relationship with her country's politics and religion becomes more complicated over time, but she tries to understand all of its history, good and bad—from the prophets and revolutionaries who inspired her to the conquerors and imperialists who have harmed Iran's people in one way or another. Marji's desire to learn and understand everything about her country contrasts strongly with the Islamic regime's plan to eliminate all culture and history except that which lines up with its conservative religious ideals.

ARGUMENT TWO

The author's second argument explains how foreign cultural influences offer a unique way to create her identity in post-Revolution Iran: "Much of what the Islamic regime wishes to eliminate from Iran's culture comes from the influences of the United Kingdom and the United States, but Marji embraces the colonizers' culture and uses it to rebel against the repressive ideology of the Islamic Revolution."

Much of what the Islamic regime wishes to eliminate from Iran's culture comes from the influences of the United Kingdom and the United States, but Marji embraces the colonizers' culture and uses it to rebel against the repressive ideology of the Islamic Revolution. Marji eagerly adopts British and American pop culture into her lifestyle. She wears jeans, decorates her room with posters of her favorite rock bands, and sneaks out of the house to buy music tapes. All of these things could get

Marji and her parents in serious trouble, but she uses them to express herself and take out her frustrations. Marji is frustrated not only with her parents but also with Iran's oppressive government. She knows the United Kingdom and the United States have interfered with her country's politics and that many Iranians suffered under the rule of the shah, whom the Western powers supported. But she disagrees with the Islamic regime's view of Iran's history and what kind of nation Iran should be in the future.

British and American culture provides a way for Marji to express that disagreement and forge her own unique cultural identity in the process. Marji is able to separate the interference of the British and American governments from the huge influence their cultures have around the world. In contrast, the Islamic regime chooses a much narrower cultural identity in response to the unwanted influence of foreign powers. The regime wants to outlaw all culture that isn't both Iranian and Islamic, with severe consequences for anyone who objects. This response alienates many of Iran's people, including Marji, who may have preferred to build a postcolonial identity that includes both traditional Iranian and Western influences.

ARGUMENT THREE

The author's final argument views the graphic novel's conclusion as a metaphor that supports the thesis: "Marji's departure for Austria serves as a metaphor for her new cultural identity—one that is forged from aspects of the cultures that have influenced her but is different from all of them."

Marji's departure for Austria serves as a metaphor for her new cultural identity—one that is forged from aspects of the cultures that have influenced her but is different from all of them. By age 14, Marji has learned about many political perspectives and experienced the clash of Iranian and Western cultures in her native city of Tehran. Her parents, Ebi and Taji, represent the old Iranian culture that Marji cherishes, but they will not always be able to protect her. The Islamic regime represents the future of Iran, purged of much of the influence of Western culture and also guarded against any new influences from other countries. Over the course of the graphic novel, Marji has created a cultural identity for herself that is different from both of these facets of Iran, and this alienates her from her own country.

Marji's journey to Austria comes precisely at the time in her life when she has found an identity she is comfortable with, in contrast to the confusion she often experienced when she was younger. By the end of the graphic novel, Marji routinely speaks out against her teachers and the Islamic regime. She says, "I was fourteen and a rebel. Nothing scared me anymore."[4] Satrapi uses visual cues to express this coming of age as well. While Satrapi consistently draws other characters with simple lines, Marji's clothing and hair become expressive and unique toward the end of the book. Marji's appearance, too, grows to resemble her mother rather than the face of the child she was at the beginning of her story. This change is another way in which Satrapi shows her growth into young adulthood. Marji's resemblance to her mother, combined with her preference for Western clothing and style, highlights her multicultural identity.

All of these cues begin to appear in the last few pages of the graphic novel, coinciding with Marji's parents' announcement that they will send her to Austria. In this way, *Persepolis* draws on a long tradition among coming-of-age stories in which protagonists must venture out into a wider world once they have accomplished a certain rite of passage. For Marji, that test was to decide what kind of person she wished to be in a country so torn between warring cultures and political ideas.

Persepolis offers the unique perspective of a young girl caught at the intersection of history, religion, politics, and colonialism in the 1900s. By combining the influences of both the colonizing and the colonized nations, Marji creates an identity for herself that is flexible, intricate, and incompatible with the post-Revolution government's policies. Iran's ancient civilization and its modern political revolutionaries provide Marji with a strong foundation for her personal identity, while the rebellious individualism in British and American pop culture offer her a way to express that identity in protest against the oppression of the Islamic regime. By the time Marji leaves Iran, she has become a representative of a younger generation of Iranians. Marji is torn—though she knows she is unsafe, she doesn't necessarily want to leave her country and her family behind. In the end, she is willing to embrace her cultural history and continue learning from it as she begins a new, international journey.

CONCLUSION

In the conclusion, the author summarizes the thesis and arguments to show that Marji has created a new identity and will be prepared for her new life.

THINKING CRITICALLY

Now it's your turn to assess the essay. Consider these questions:

1. Iran's Islamic regime develops an "us versus them" mentality that relies on portraying different or "other" people as dangerous to Iranian society. Marxists, Iraqis, and even Marji and her family sometimes fall into this group. Can you think of more groups of people who might be considered "others" by the Islamic regime?
2. Postcolonial criticism often examines the role of the literary canon in separating people and cultures from each other. A canon can be based on cultural or ethnic groups (the Western canon), but it can also be based on a literary medium (a canon of graphic novels). Given Marji's multifaceted cultural identity, do you think *Persepolis* belongs (or should belong) to a literary canon?
3. At the end of *Persepolis*, Marji seems emotionally conflicted about leaving her home, even though it has become unsafe for her to stay in Iran because of who she is. Why might she experience these conflicting emotions, and what does it say about her multicultural identity?

OTHER APPROACHES

The previous essay is only one example of how to analyze the graphic novel *Persepolis*. Another approach might examine the story from a feminist perspective. Yet another option is to focus on the graphic novel's portrayal of Marxist themes.

Feminist Criticism

In *Persepolis*, Iran's Islamic regime claims women tempt and corrupt men with their bodies, and this is why women must cover themselves from head to toe. The regime also relies on men for the troops it needs to fight the war against Iraq. Feminism opposes not only the oppression of women but also the indoctrination of men as participants in the patriarchy. A reading of *Persepolis* from a feminist perspective could be: Because the Islamic regime relies on a religious tradition of mistrust between men and women to hold on to its power, the form of feminism expressed by Marji, her mother, and other Iranian women is not only a movement for gender equality in Iran but also a revolutionary movement to end the war with Iraq and replace Iran's oppressive regime.

Marxist Criticism

Karl Marx and the political philosophy he developed are a constant presence in *Persepolis*, both because Marji's parents hold Marxist views but also because in the years leading to the Islamic Revolution, many Iranians sought a more equal form of government than the shah's oppressive regime. A thesis from a Marxist perspective could be: Marji's parents and her uncle Anoosh fight for equality, but *Persepolis* shows that the Marxist class struggle must continue because Iran's Islamic regime strongly resembles the oppressive government it replaced.

8

OVERVIEWS OF *MAUS* AND *MARCH*

Maus: A Survivor's Tale: Volume I: My Father Bleeds History, written and illustrated by Art Spiegelman, is a 1986 graphic novel that tells the story of the author's father, Vladek Spiegelman, a Polish Jew who survived the Holocaust. *Maus* takes its title, the German word for "mouse," from the author's depiction of Jews as mice and the Nazis as cats.

Maus features two narratives. One explores the author's relationship with his father, while the other recounts Vladek's experiences in the ghettos the Nazis established after invading Poland

Approximately 6 million Jews were killed during the Holocaust.

in September 1939. The author, Art, weaves these two stories together by depicting a series of visits to his father's home in New York City in 1978. Vladek's somewhat wandering stories about himself tend to frustrate Art, who seems focused on learning about World War II and the Holocaust. But these stories offer the reader a more complete picture of Vladek as an intensely proud survivor of the worst genocide in human history.

Vladek and Anja

Vladek narrates his story to Art, who writes everything down. Vladek begins by telling his son about his life in Poland, years before the Nazi invasion. He had his own small textile business in the town of Czestochowa. One day he traveled to the nearby town of Sosnowiec and met a young woman named Anja. They quickly fell in love and got married.

Anja's family was wealthy, and her father gave Vladek money to open a textile factory. Soon after it opened, Vladek and Anja had their first child, Richieu, in October 1937. They were overjoyed, but their happiness was short-lived. Anti-Semitic riots had begun in Poland. Vladek explains to Art that most Polish people believed

Vladek rides an exercise bike while telling his son about his past.

Adolf Hitler and the Nazis only wanted to take back small parts of Polish territory—areas that had been part of Germany prior to World War I (1914–1918).

War in Poland

In August 1939, Vladek received a draft notice from the Polish government. Meanwhile, Anja and Richieu fled back to Sosnowiec. After only a few days of military training, Vladek found himself in the trenches. He killed a German soldier, but the Germans won the battle. Vladek was taken to a prisoner of war camp where he first experienced the cruelty of the Nazis. They forced the prisoners to work and gave them very little rest, shelter, or food.

After weeks of this forced labor, the Nazis sent Vladek and other prisoners home. But on the way back to Poland, Vladek's train did not stop in Sosnowiec. It continued onward to Warsaw, the capital of Poland. When Vladek got off the train, he discovered that the Nazis had executed 600 other prisoners of war—mostly Jews—just before he had arrived. Fearing the same would happen to him, Vladek arranged an escape and returned to his family in Sosnowiec. But soon, the Germans required all Jews to register and depart for Srodula, a small village that became the Jewish ghetto outside Sosnowiec.

Inside the Ghettos

Vladek and Anja sent their son, Richieu, to another town with Anja's sister, Tosha. But the Nazis soon overtook that ghetto too. Rather than be sent to the gas chambers, Tosha killed Richieu and then committed suicide.

Vladek, Anja, and their remaining family devised clever ways of evading the Nazis. Sometimes they hid in disguised bunkers in the ghettos. Other times they wandered the countryside, taking shelter in abandoned buildings. But eventually the Nazis caught them. Vladek

Millions of families were separated during the Holocaust.

and Anja were sent to Auschwitz, a concentration and extermination camp. Vladek tells Art he never expected to leave Auschwitz alive.

Over the course of the graphic novel, Art learns that his mother, Anja, kept a diary. Art asks Vladek to look for it around the house because it would be helpful to Art in writing his story. Finally, as Vladek tells Art how they came to Auschwitz, he remembers that he burned Anja's diary after she committed suicide in 1968. Art is furious. He calls his father a murderer for destroying his mother's record of her time during the Holocaust. Art quickly apologizes, but as the graphic novel ends, he still feels anger toward his father.

Marching toward Equality

March: Book One is a graphic novel written by John Lewis and Andrew Aydin and illustrated by Nate Powell. Published in 2013, *March* is an autobiographical work recounting the early life of US Congressman John Lewis and his experiences with the civil rights movement during the late 1950s and early 1960s. Much like *Maus*, Lewis frames his history inside another story about the present day—his life as a congressman and the inauguration of Barack Obama, the first African-American president of the United States.

The graphic novel begins in Washington, DC, on January 20, 2009. Congressman John Lewis prepares for the historic day ahead of him. On this day, Barack Obama will be inaugurated as president. Lewis first makes a stop at his congressional office, where he meets with his assistant Andrew Aydin. As they get ready to head to the Capitol, a woman knocks on the office door. She says she and her two sons have come from Georgia to see the inauguration, but they wanted to stop by the congressman's office first. Lewis offers to tell his three visitors about his experiences in the civil rights movement.

A Childhood in Alabama

Lewis grew up on a farm in Pike County, Alabama. As a child, he was fascinated with chickens and took great care of them. He was also interested in faith and religion, and he held sermons, baptisms, and funerals for his chickens. Though his parents wanted him to stay home and work on the farm, Lewis would hide and wait for the school bus to come by and jump onto it at the last second. This early interest in education was one of the things that led him to participate in the civil rights movement.

In 1954, during Lewis's freshman year of high school, the US Supreme Court ruled that segregation was illegal. A few months later, Lewis was listening to the radio and heard Dr. Martin Luther King Jr. speak for the first time. King's speech united Lewis's interest in religion and his belief that segregation was wrong.

Civil Rights and Lunch Counter Sit-Ins

Lewis began attending workshops on nonviolent protest led by a college student named Jim Lawson. Lewis and several friends soon created the Nashville Student Movement, an organization that focused on ways to resist fighting back when people threatened them.

In November 1959, Lewis and his fellow protesters began "sitting in" at the lunch counters in local department stores. The stores charged black customers and white customers the same prices for goods, but black people were not allowed to eat at the stores' lunch counters. By purchasing an item in the stores and then sitting down at the lunch counter, the protesters peacefully demonstrated against the blatant unfairness and racism.

These first few protests went well. Many white students joined in to support their classmates' struggle for equality. Sometimes the department stores closed the lunch counter and turned out the lights. Other times angry crowds of white people showed up and insulted them. But Lewis and the other protesters did not waver.

The Civil Rights Movement Grows

As the protesters' numbers swelled to hundreds of participants, the backlash from the police and prejudiced white southerners increased. Groups of young white people came into the stores during the sit-ins and beat up the protesters. The police stood by and allowed the beatings, then rushed in afterward to arrest the protesters who chose to stay in the stores.

Lewis reflects on the nonviolent approach to fighting for civil rights.

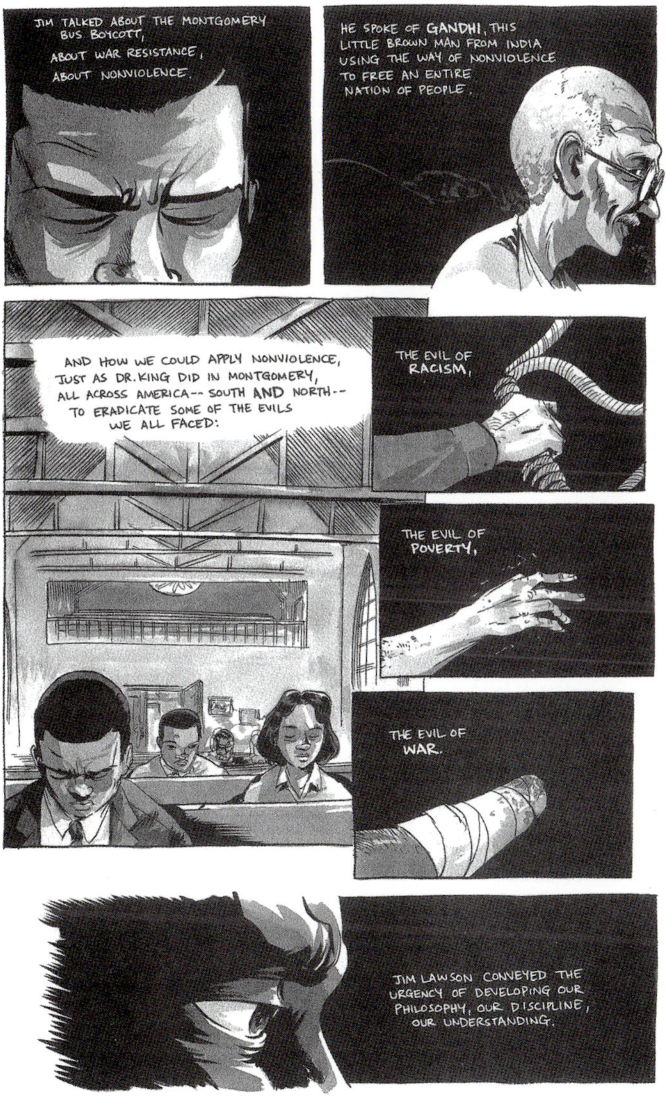

At one event, 82 protesters went to jail and refused to pay bail. When a judge ordered them to each pay a fine of $50, they also refused. The protesters believed paying fines or bail would be participating in the system of discrimination that had led to segregation in the first place. So the judge instead ordered them to serve 30 days in a workhouse. But this triggered an even stronger response from others around the country. Under pressure, the city released the protesters from their sentence early.

Violence escalated against prominent protesters. But overall, the backlash seemed only to strengthen the movement. After one of their the leaders was dismissed from his professorship, dozens of fellow teachers and staff threatened to resign in protest. When another civil rights leader's home was bombed, thousands of people gathered at city hall in Nashville to tell the mayor to end segregation in their city. *March: Book One* ends with King delivering a speech in Nashville. On May 10, 1960, the downtown department stores finally served lunch to their black customers.

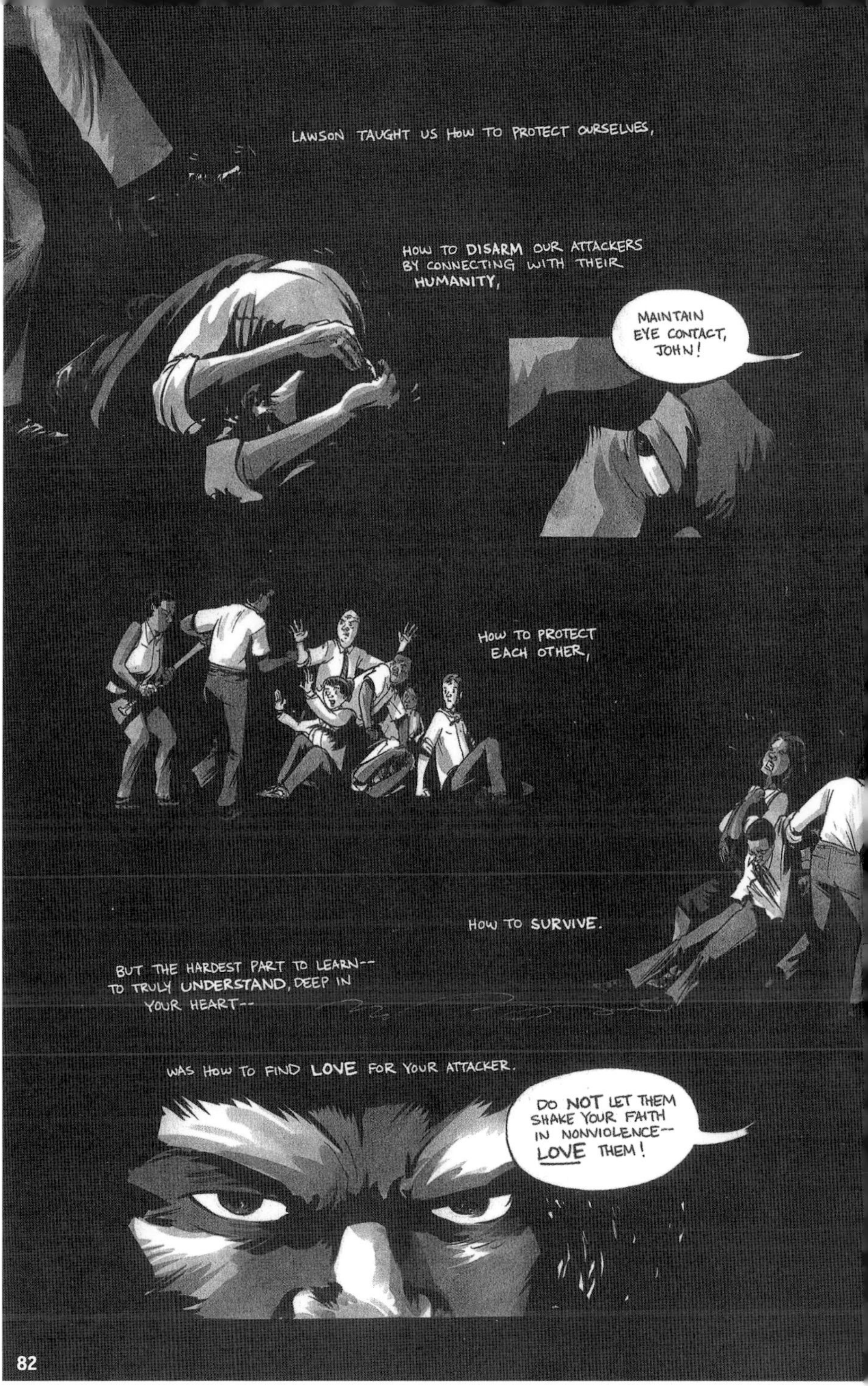

The nonviolent movement focused on the idea that love is more powerful than hate.

9

INCOMPLETE UNDERSTANDING

Maus and *March* are examples of the memoir genre of graphic novels. They tell the story of true historical events from the perspective of someone who lived through them. The authors of *Maus* and *March* both tell their stories through a frame story, a narrative that sets another narrative within itself. In *Maus*, Art Spiegelman serves as an intermediary between Vladek and the reader, while *March* relies on John Lewis to tell his story. But both graphic novels present their protagonists, Vladek and Lewis, as the sole source of information about not only their personal experiences, but also the historical events in which they took part.

Postmodernist criticism examines the breakdown of our languages and the ways in which we make sense of the world. In literature, postmodernism often

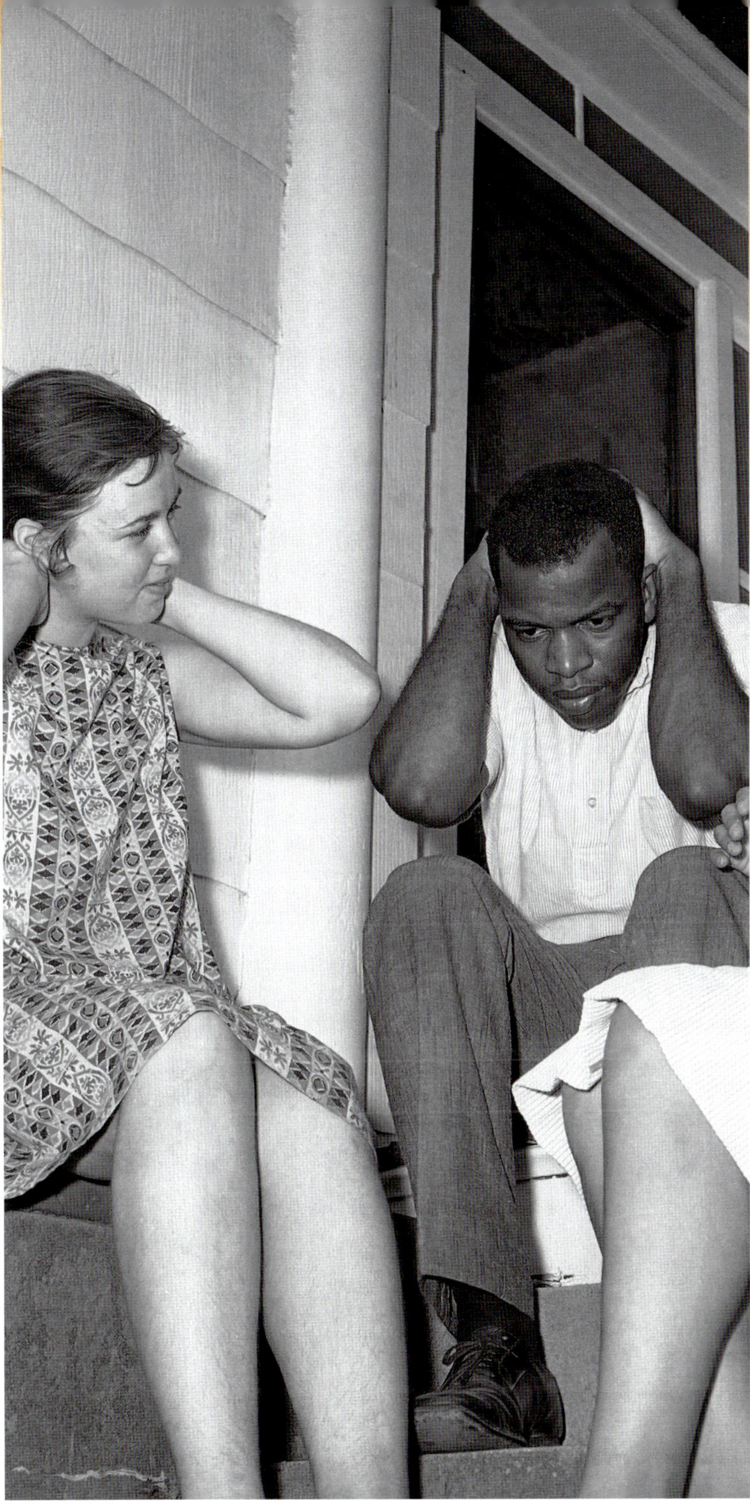

Lewis showed protesters how to protect themselves in 1963.

takes issue with the narrative, which forces readers to understand the text in a specific way, and with the author, who tries to express meanings that may be impossible to express through written language. *Maus* and *March* both attempt to explain complicated and traumatic events through a single person who participated in them. But because the reader is separated from these events by layers of interpretation—including the protagonist, the author, and the graphic novel medium itself—the reader's understanding of the events of *Maus* and *March* will always be incomplete.

Though Vladek and Lewis both attempt to relate their experiences as accurately as they can, language inevitably fails them. Postmodernism emphasizes that the meanings of words are

THESIS STATEMENT

The thesis statement outlines the main argument for the essay: "But because the reader is separated from these events by layers of interpretation—including the protagonist, the author, and the graphic novel medium itself—the reader's understanding of the events of *Maus* and *March* will always be incomplete."

ARGUMENT ONE

The first argument discusses Vladek and Lewis's difficulties in fully describing their experiences: "Though Vladek and Lewis both attempt to relate their experiences as accurately as they can, language inevitably fails them."

subjective. They are often inadequate to express even simple meanings, much less describe such complicated events as the Holocaust or the civil rights movement. Lewis says he felt "free" and "liberated" while being arrested for protesting at the Nashville lunch counters, but his words seem to contradict what's actually happening to him.[1] How can he feel "free" while being arrested, when going to jail is the opposite of freedom? Postmodernism argues there are no words in the English language for Lewis to accurately describe his feelings at that moment, so he is forced to use unusual and even contradictory words to express himself in the context of such an intense experience.

Vladek Spiegelman seems to encounter similar failures of language, but he handles them in a different way. He describes them matter-of-factly, without any mention of his emotional reactions. When he tells Art about Richieu's death, he calls it a "tragedy among tragedies," as if he is reporting the news.[2] Regarding Vladek and Anja's arrival at Auschwitz, Vladek says, "We knew the stories—that they will gas us and throw us in the ovens. This was 1944. We knew everything. And here we were."[3] There is no mention of fear, sadness, or horror—any or all of which would be common things to feel at the gates of Auschwitz. Vladek's words, "here we were," are incapable of expressing what he and Anja experienced there.

Art himself reflects this failure of the language back to his father. When Vladek has finished his story, Art simply says, "My God."[4] Vladek seems to take Art's words as an expression of sympathy, but a postmodernist reader might interpret them differently: as a placeholder, a way for Art to say that words fail him as he tries to imagine what the experience must have been like for his father. In *Maus* and *March*'s descriptions of ordinary people in extraordinary circumstances, these failures of language mean the reader can only guess the full extent of the narrator's meaning.

ARGUMENT TWO

The second argument examines how the author(s) of each novel might affect the reader's understanding: "The authors of *Maus* and *March* stand as another layer of interpretation between the reader and the historical events."

The authors of *Maus* and *March* stand as another layer of interpretation between the reader and the historical events. Before an author even begins writing, he or she makes decisions that will shape the finished product: which events to include, which to leave out, whose perspective the story will take, and so on. For example, in *Maus*, Art only wants to hear about those events that interest him, and he seems to want to hear about them in perfectly chronological order. On several occasions throughout the graphic novel, he becomes frustrated by his father's digressions and distractions as he tells his story. Art becomes a sort of gatekeeper who decides which information and how much of it will reach the reader. On the other hand, Art is furious when his father reveals that some information, such as Anja's diary, is no longer accessible. Art's frustration with his father likely influences how he portrays Vladek, which may act as a "lens" that obscures the real Vladek from the reader's view.

March does not feature an intermediary author within the narrative. The story is told by Lewis himself. However, Lewis's adviser Andrew Aydin is also credited as a cowriter of the graphic novel. Aydin appears briefly in a scene in Congressman Lewis's office, but for the most part he is merely a name on the book's cover. This means the reader knows almost nothing about Aydin and how he might have influenced the story that *March* tells. With Art Spiegelman's depiction of himself in *Maus*, the reader can get a sense of the relationship between Art the author and Vladek the storyteller—but in *March*, the reader has no way to access or understand what perspectives Aydin might be bringing to the graphic novel.

ARGUMENT THREE

The final argument explores how the graphic novel medium might interfere with the story's accuracy: "Though the graphic novel's visual presentation may seem to be a more complete or expressive way of narrating historical events, the medium still has limitations."

Though the graphic novel's visual presentation may seem to be a more complete or expressive way of narrating historical events, the medium still has limitations. Graphic novels can show instead of tell the reader about events, but the images are not photographs. Each panel was carefully drawn by someone trying to capture a particular moment in time. The reader has no way of knowing whether these moments were captured accurately, nor does the reader know why the illustrators arranged each panel the way they did. Further, the panels are limited to a snapshot of the events and the people who took part in them. People have a wide range of emotions and reactions to their experiences, and the comic format can show only one of those emotions at any given time. One panel might emphasize a specific emotion for its dramatic impact on the story but neglect other important emotions the character might have experienced.

For example, when Lewis narrates the incidents of February 27, 1960, in which he and the other sit-in protesters were attacked by angry white mobs, the illustrations show the protesters feeling sadness and pain as they are beaten and humiliated. Meanwhile, the white attackers look angry, enraged at the black protesters. But it is unreasonable to assume these are the only emotions the people experienced. Might the protesters have also felt angry and wished they could fight back? Similarly, might their attackers have been ashamed of their actions but afraid to show it? *March*'s illustrations can offer the reader only one truth at a time. A postmodernist reading argues there are many truths available in every situation, and which truth the illustrations choose to show has an impact on the reader's understanding of the events.

Maus introduces another complication by depicting its characters as animals rather than as humans. The animals' faces are simple and cartoonish, making it difficult for the characters to display complex human emotions. Furthermore, *Maus*'s characters are separated by species—Jews are mice, Germans are cats, and Poles are pigs. Even relatively simple emotions such as anger, sadness, or happiness might look different from each other depending on Spiegelman's style of drawing each animal. These differences could drastically change how the reader views the characters. In both *Maus* and *March*, simple snapshots of faces and their surroundings are incapable of expressing a complete picture of people's experiences.

The Holocaust and the American civil rights movement were extremely complicated events that permanently changed the lives of millions of people. *Maus* and *March* attempt to explain a single perspective on each of these events through Vladek Spiegelman and John Lewis, but their experiences are subjective, limited, and ultimately incapable of offering more than a narrow snapshot of a story larger than themselves. A postmodernist perspective on these novels reveals layers of interpretation—including the narrator, the authors, and the medium itself—that influence the reader's understanding of these events.

CONCLUSION

The conclusion restates the thesis and summarizes the arguments that support it.

THINKING CRITICALLY

Now it's your turn to assess the essay. Consider these questions:

1. Can you find any evidence that disproves the author's thesis?
2. Can you find any other layers of interpretation that may alter or interfere with these portrayals of historical events?
3. Do you notice any gaps, or events that seem to be missing from the narratives? How might those gaps change the reader's understanding of the Holocaust or the civil rights movement?

OTHER APPROACHES

The previous essay is only one way to examine the graphic novels *Maus* and *March*. Another approach might choose to explore the graphic novels from a feminist perspective. Still another option might be to focus on critical race theory.

Feminist Criticism

Maus and *March* both rely almost solely on the experiences of men to describe their historical events, despite the fact that women played an equal part in both Vladek's survival of the Holocaust and Lewis's struggle for civil rights in the United States. A feminist reading of *Maus* and *March* could be: Neither *Maus* nor *March* offers a detailed perspective from women who participated in these historical events, reinforcing the patriarchal assumption that history and society are primarily focused around men and their experiences.

Critical Race Theory

Maus and *March* both narrate historical events that were centered around their society's perceptions of race and ethnicity. These perceptions of Jews in Nazi Germany and African Americans in the segregated American South were largely based on stereotypes of a marginalized group of people. A reading of these graphic novels from a critical race theory perspective could be: While Spiegelman's depiction of his father in *Maus* sometimes reinforces stereotypes about the Jewish people, *March* seems to actively resist such stereotypes of African Americans.

ANALYZE IT!

Now that you have learned different approaches to analyzing a work, are you ready to perform your own analysis? You have read that this type of evaluation can help you look at literature in a new way and make you pay attention to certain issues you may not have otherwise recognized. So, why not use one of these approaches to consider a fresh take on your favorite work?

First, choose a philosophy, critical theory, or other approach and consider which work or works you want to analyze. Remember the approach you choose is a springboard for asking questions about the works.

Next, write a specific question that relates to your approach or philosophy. Then you can form your thesis, which should provide the answer to that question. Your thesis is the most important part of your analysis and offers an argument about the work, considering its characters, plot, or literary techniques, or what it says about society or the world. Recall that the thesis statement typically appears at the very end of the introductory paragraph of your essay. It is usually only one sentence long.

After you have written your thesis, find evidence to back it up. Good places to start are in the work itself or in journals or articles that discuss what other people have said about it. You may also want to read about the author or creator's life so you can get a sense of what factors may have affected the creative process. This can be especially useful if you are considering how the work connects to history or the author's intent.

You should also explore parts of the book that seem to disprove your thesis and create an argument against them. As you do this, you might want to address what others have written about the book. Their quotes may help support your claim.

Before you start analyzing a work, think about the different arguments made in this book. Reflect on how evidence supporting the thesis was presented. Did you find that some of the techniques used to back up the arguments were more convincing than others? Try these methods as you prove your thesis in your own analysis paper.

When you are finished writing your analysis, read it over carefully. Is your thesis statement understandable? Do the supporting arguments flow logically, with the topic of each paragraph clearly stated? Can you add any information that would present your readers with a stronger argument in favor of your thesis? Were you able to use quotes from the book, as well as from other critics, to enhance your ideas?

Did you see the work in a new light?

GLOSSARY

ANAGRAM
A word, phrase, or name formed by rearranging the letters of another.

BINARY
Something that relates to, is composed of, or involves two things.

CIVIL RIGHTS
Enforceable privileges of citizens to personal and political liberties such as freedom of speech, the right to vote, and social equality.

COLONIALISM
The practice of gaining political control over another country, occupying it with settlers, and exploiting its resources.

COMMUNIST
Having to do with a system in which the government controls the economy and owns all property.

FEMINISM
The belief that women should have the same opportunities and rights as men politically, socially, and economically.

FUNDAMENTALIST
Having to do with a form of religion that strictly adheres to a literal interpretation of scripture.

GHETTO
A section of a town or city in which people of a certain race, religion, or ethnic group are forced to live.

IMPERIALISM
A policy in which a country attempts to increase its power through military force and by controlling colonies in other parts of the world.

INDOCTRINATE
To teach someone to fully accept the ideas, opinions, and beliefs of a particular group and not to consider other ideas, opinions, or beliefs.

MARGINALIZE
To exclude a person or group of people or treat them as unimportant or of a lower class.

MARXISM
A political philosophy, developed in the 1800s by Karl Marx and Friedrich Engels, that examines the relationships between social classes and the materials produced in a society.

PANEL
A single image within a comic strip, usually framed by lines or borders.

PATRIARCHY
A society in which men dominate.

POSTCOLONIALIST
Having to do with an academic discipline that analyzes, explains, and responds to the cultural legacy of colonialism and imperialism.

POSTMODERNISM
A style in the arts, architecture, and criticism that distrusts ideologies and argues against the idea of a singular truth.

PURGATORY
In religious doctrines, a place or state of suffering inhabited by the souls of sinners who must atone for their sins before moving on to heaven.

SEGREGATION
The practice of separating groups of people based on race, gender, ethnicity, or other factors.

STEREOTYPE
An often unfair and untrue belief that many people have about all people or things with a particular characteristic—for example, gender or race.

ADDITIONAL
RESOURCES

SELECTED BIBLIOGRAPHY

Lemire, Jeff, and Dustin Nguyen. *Descender: Tin Stars*. Berkeley, CA: Image Comics, 2015. Print.

Lewis, John, Andrew Aydin, and Nate Powell. *March: Book One*. Marietta, GA: Top Shelf Productions, 2013. Print.

Satrapi, Marjane. *Persepolis: The Story of a Childhood*. New York: Pantheon, 2003. Print.

Spiegelman, Art. *Maus: A Survivor's Tale: Volume I: My Father Bleeds History*. New York: Pantheon, 1986. Print.

Stevenson, Noelle, Grace Ellis, and Brooke Allen. *Lumberjanes: Beware the Kitten Holy*. Los Angeles: BOOM! Box, 2015. Print.

FURTHER READINGS

Lewis, John, Andrew Aydin, and Nate Powell. *March: Book Two*. Marietta, GA: Top Shelf Productions, 2015. Print.

Satrapi, Marjane. *Persepolis 2: The Story of a Return*. New York: Pantheon, 2004. Print.

Spiegelman, Art. *Co-mix: A Retrospective of Comics, Graphics, and Scraps*. Montreal: Drawn & Quarterly, 2013. Print.

Spiegelman, Art. *Maus: A Survivor's Tale: Volume II: And Here My Troubles Began*. New York: Pantheon, 1991. Print.

Weiner, Stephen. *Faster Than a Speeding Bullet: The Rise of the Graphic Novel*. 2nd ed. New York: NBM, 2012. Print.

WEBSITES

To learn more about Essential Literary Genres, visit **booklinks.abdopublishing.com**. These links are routinely monitored and updated to provide the most current information available.

FOR MORE INFORMATION

For more information on this subject, contact or visit the following organizations:

Comic Book Legal Defense Fund
811 SW Naito Parkway, Suite 100
Portland, OR 97204
971-266-8212
http://www.cbldf.org
The Comic Book Legal Defense Fund is an organization that fights for the First Amendment rights of those involved in comics.

Society of Illustrators
128 East 63rd Street
New York, NY 10065
212-838-2560
http://www.societyillustrators.org
The Society of Illustrators holds exhibitions and promotes the art of illustration.

University Library
University of Illinois at Urbana-Champaign
1408 W Gregory Drive
Urbana, IL 61801
217-333-2290
http://www.library.illinois.edu/ugl/about/graphic_novels.html
The library at the University of Illinois houses more than 2,000 graphic novels from around the world. Many are in their original language, and others have been translated into English.

SOURCE NOTES

CHAPTER 1. INTRODUCTION TO LITERARY GENRES

None.

CHAPTER 2. AN OVERVIEW OF *DESCENDER: TIN STARS*

None.

CHAPTER 3. WORKING-CLASS HEROES

None.

CHAPTER 4. AN OVERVIEW OF *LUMBERJANES: BEWARE THE KITTEN HOLY*

1. Noelle Stevenson, Grace Ellis, and Brooke Allen. *Lumberjanes: Beware the Kitten Holy*. Los Angeles, BOOM! Box, 2015. Print. 13.

2. Ibid. 100.

CHAPTER 5. DIVERSE GENDER IDENTITIES

None.

CHAPTER 6. AN OVERVIEW OF *PERSEPOLIS*

1. Marjane Satrapi. *Persepolis: The Story of a Childhood*. New York: Pantheon, 2003. Print. 8.

CHAPTER 7. POSTCOLONIAL IDENTITY

1. Marjane Satrapi. *Persepolis: The Story of a Childhood*. New York: Pantheon, 2003. Print. 6.
2. Ibid. 8.
3. Ibid. 13.
4. Ibid. 143.

CHAPTER 8. OVERVIEWS OF *MAUS* AND *MARCH*

None.

CHAPTER 9. INCOMPLETE UNDERSTANDING

1. John Lewis, Andrew Aydin, and Nate Powell. *March: Book One*. Marietta, GA: Top Shelf Productions, 2013. Print. 102.
2. Art Spiegelman. *Maus: A Survivor's Tale: Volume I: My Father Bleeds History*. New York: Pantheon, 1986. Print. 109.
3. Ibid. 157.
4. Ibid. 158.

INDEX

ABOUT THE AUTHOR

Andrew Dale holds a bachelor of arts degree in English and German from Hamline University. He has presented research on J. R. R. Tolkien's *The Lord of the Rings* and medieval Irish mythology at national conferences. Andrew's favorite graphic novel is *Batman: Year 100*. He lives in Minneapolis, Minnesota, with his wife, Lindsay, and their dog, Samwise.